Ko Olina

Place of Joy

Ko Olina

RESORT & MARINA
HONOLULU, HAWAII

Ko Olina Resort Association
92-1480 Alii Nui Drive
Honolulu, Hawaii 96707
(808) 680-7680
www.koolina.com

Copyright © 2002
Belknap Publishing & Design
P.O. Box 22387
Honolulu, HI 96823
A Resort Publications® book

Text & photographs ©2002 by Rita Ariyoshi
Hawaiian stories ©2002 by Jodi Parry Belknap
Painting, p.40 ©2002 by Michael Furuya
Additional photograph credits on p. 64

Cover Design: Buzz Belknap
Book Design: Jodi Parry Belknap

Library of Congress Cataloging-in-Publication Data
ISBN 0-9723420-2-8

Printed in China

Ko Olina Resort & Marina in 2000.
*Designed to become Hawaii's premiere 21st -
century travel destination, Ko Olina is a carefully
planned expanse of prime beachfront acreage on
the dry, sunny West Beach side of the Island of
Oahu. Nestled against the cooling shades of the
Waianae Mountain Range, its features now
include a deep draft harbor, full-service marina,
four swimming lagoons, championship golf
course and club house, luxury homes,
condominiums and hotel, elegant wedding
chapels and indoor/outdoor function venues.*

Ko Olina
Place of Joy

Written and photographed by Rita Ariyoshi
Hawaiian stories by Jodi Parry Belknap

Preface

Family trees are treasured because they tell us who we are, who we came from, and who comes after us. We see that we are part of a wonderful story. We savor the ancestral names and choose them again and again for our children, giving them roots and a sense of belonging to something greater than themselves.

Hawaii is one of the few places in the world where people come to love the place with the same passion and devotion usually reserved for a person. The Hawaiians expressed this *aloha aina*, love of the land, by naming every valley, mountain, rock and temple. They had countless names for rain and wind, depending on their subtle variations. And every place had its history and legends.

When Ko Olina was conceived as a resort, the developers knew the importance of choosing the right name. They consulted the late Reverend Abraham Akaka, *Kahu* (pastor) of Kawaiahao Church in Honolulu. Reverend Akaka proposed Ko Olina, which means place or fulfillment of joy, simply because that was the ancestral name, the true name. It just happened, in the Hawaiian way, to be prophetic of the place's destiny.

In this book, we share the history of Ko Olina and its legends. Many stories found in the book have never been written down before, but were told from generation to generation among the people who lived here. Other parts of the book were gathered from many sources and woven together for the first time into a cohesive unit. We've included *moolelo* in each chapter. These are stories regarded by many as myths, but like most great legends, they grew from truth and contain wisdom. Two legends are brand new, but like the great stories of old, are based on actual events and traditions. In gathering and setting down all these elements, we add our own chapters to carry the story of Ko Olina forward.

A me ke aloha pumehana,

Jeffrey R. Stone, President, Ko Olina Resort Association, Principal, Ko Olina Companies LLC

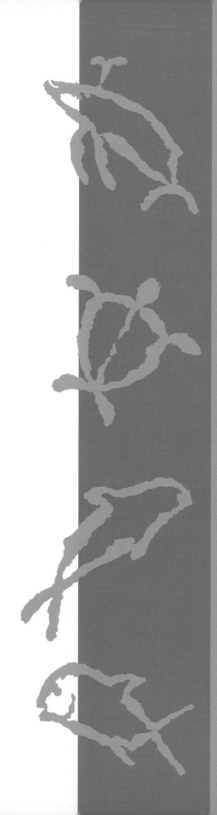

Contents

Introduction

Ko Olina is my sanctuary, the place where I feel secure. The Hawaiian word for it is *nanea*. I am nanea when I walk the grounds of Ko Olina. I feel really good, invigorated. My head clears, even if the day is hot. The feeling is so deep in my soul that it's hard to explain.

When I was a little girl growing up at Ko Olina, my mother Lei Fernandez used to sit in the water of the cove at Lanikuhonua and call to the fish and they'd come swimming in, so many of them, all their mouths above the water, hungry to be fed. My brother Sonny and I would pick up the fish in our hands and kiss them and rub their shiny cheeks.

Ko Olina is like my church, the coconut trees holding up the cathedral of the sky.

When I was given the text of this book to read, I brought it to bed with me, and in the quiet, with the sound of the Pacific softly in the background, I settled in with it. As I read, all my feelings for this very special place gathered around me and I was nanea. The book captures all that I feel about Ko Olina. The Hawaiian stories woven throughout brought me back to my childhood when the world was full of magic.

I hope everyone who reads this book will find as much pleasure in it as I did.

Lynette "Nettie" Tiffany, Kahu, Lanikuhonua, The Estate of James Campbell

View of the Waianae Mountains *from a lagoon at Lanikuhonua, the private Estate of James Campbell at Ko Olina.*

Beginnings

The dream of Ko Olina, the Place of Joy, is as ancient as Paradise. Since the dawn of time, the human soul has needed a radiant vision, our spirits require simple goodness, and our bodies yearn for pleasure and peace, a place of joy. The concept of Paradise is integral to who we are; it comes in the bones as memory or a quiet stirring that whispers to each of us. We seek that place of joy as deer long for running streams and flowers drink sunlight. And when we find our place of joy, we know it; we recognize its contours. We feel its sweet breath. Ko Olina. The name is prophetic.

Three and a half million years ago, thousands of miles from land, far from any eyes that might see it, a turbulence appeared in the vast calm of the Pacific, as if a pot were promising to boil. The immensity of waters gathered, bubbled, churned. Great billows of steam rose and ascended in white columns towering over the waves, invading the flawless blue sky. Suddenly, with a mighty roar, a volcano broke the chains of the sea in a cataclysm of fire. Flames erupted from the water in a terrifying and beautiful passion as if the ocean itself was on fire. The inferno hurled rocks and lava high against the heavens as it brought forth new land from the womb of the planet. Oahu was born on that distant morning.

The volcano was called Waianae. It kept erupting and climbing until it reached eight thousand feet above the sea. A million years went by, and another volcano, Koolau, rose from the waves, its voluminous lava pooling against Waianae's older slopes, joining the two massive seamounts into one large island. A mere twenty thousand years ago, Koolau gasped out a tuff cone that came to be called Diamond Head because of the glittering volcanic rocks festooning its crater.

It's hard to imagine a world without Hawaii, yet it is among the youngest places on Earth. The rest of the world had already settled into continents; great glaciers had advanced and retreated, carving valleys and mountains on the face of the world; the dinosaurs were extinct; and the ancestors of man were walking about, when a rift opened in the floor of the Pacific spilling forth fire and lava the color of blood. The flames from the molten core of the planet were so hot they raged in the dense cold oceanic depths. The lava piled up in pillows and mounds, building first one island and then another, until one hundred thirty-two of them lay like pearls upon the breast of the tropical sea. The Hawaiian archipelago stretches for 1,523 miles from Kure, the oldest island, to Loihi, the newest, still embryonic, fuming five thousand feet below the sea surface, twenty miles southeast of the island of Hawaii. Of the eight major islands, Oahu, at 608 square miles, is third largest and third oldest. It has matured and

An indigenous Hawaiian honeycreeper, the scarlet iiwi, right, grown plump on berries and beetles in the rain forest, surveys his paradisal habitat. **Opposite page: A golden amakihi** *perches high in the cool uplands.*

The Nature Conservancy of Hawaii conducts guided walks in the Honouliuli Forest Preserve above Ko Olina where hikers sometimes glimpse gloriously feathered birds such as these. Hawaiians of old used brilliant red, yellow and black feathers plucked from these birds and others to create lustrous feather capes, helmets and cloaks.

Some among many staple food sources carefully cultivated by the first Hawaiians in pre-Western times are pictured on page 13. They include, top: banana and breadfruit; bottom: coconuts and taro.

settled, as volcanic islands do. Today, the highest point of the Waianae Mountains, and of Oahu, is Mount Kaala at 4,020 feet, half its original height. Koolau's tallest peak is Mount Konahuanui. At 3,150 feet, it towers in emerald splendor over the windward side of the island.

The Hawaiian Islands are among the most isolated on the globe. They remained a secret of Nature for millions of years while rain, wind, and surf scoured and shaped them, coral reefs built shelves around them, earthquakes and catastrophic landslides dramatically sculpted them into high islands with vast amphitheater valleys such as Makaha and Waianae near Ko Olina. With no one watching, Nature had its way, delighting in extremes, creating amazingly varied environments in close proximity. Waialeale on the island of Kauai is the wettest spot on Earth. Mauna Kea on the island of Hawaii is 32,796 feet high when measured from its base on the ocean floor, taller than Everest. The sheer green palisades of Oahu's Koolau Mountains are one of the scenic wonders of the state. Rain forests, sunny lowlands, deserts, bogs, coastal dunes, and snowy peaks found themselves neighbors. Biologists have identified at least 180 separate types of habitat. Creation was extravagant, reckless and utterly beautiful in the formation of Hawaii.

All the climates of the world are represented in the islands, and within only a few miles of each other. Even though the archipelago sits comfortably in the tropics, the height of the mountains, the constant tradewinds, and the rainfall allow for this wide variation in weather. Most of the time, however, across most of the land, the climate is akin to perpetual June. This is largely due to the size of the Pacific. The huge mass of ocean functions as a temperature regulator, soothing the brunt of winter storms rolling down from the Arctic in winter, and taking the heat off the tropical summers.

The Hawaiians recognized two seasons: *kau*, or summer, which runs from May through September when the temperatures average eighty-five degrees Fahrenheit, and *hooilo*, which corresponds to winter, from October through April, when the average temperature drops to seventy-eight degrees.

It's natural that life would thrive in such a benign climate, but first life had to find the small barren islands in the heart of the ocean. The discovery was gradual. Life arrived as seeds and spores borne in the jet streams and ocean currents, on logs swept from far

continents and as gifts of migratory birds. Successful landings happened once every hundred thousand years or so.

In the loneliness of the ocean, these few original colonizing species evolved into constellations of unique plants and animals. Scientists hold that Hawaii is one of the planet's most spectacular laboratories for observing the wonders of evolution. Here, a single finch-like bird became more than forty species of Hawaiian honeycreeper, some of which live in the mountains near Ko Olina. The

humble sunflower morphed into the magnificent silversword found on mountain summits. Over ninety percent of the plants, birds and insects native to the islands are endemic, found nowhere else on Earth. Hawaii is Nature's Lost Ark.

Honouliuli, a 3,692-acre nature preserve in the Waianae mountains, today is home to nearly seventy rare and endangered plant and animal species. The scarlet apapane, wise elepaio, and golden amakihi sing in the misty forests. The pueo, the Hawaiian owl that flies by day, hovers as a guardian spirit, an *aumakua* of Ko Olina. The lovely tree snails with their colorful, intricately-patterned shells, which were once so numerous on Oahu that the tradewinds playing across their shells sounded like a symphony of flutes, still hide shyly among the dewy green leaves. The Nature Conservancy of Hawaii leads monthly hikes into this pristine area above Ko Olina so people can still enjoy the exquisite beauty of Hawaii's native forest and encounter some of the rarest biota in the world.

The first people to discover Hawaii, Polynesians who sailed from lands thousands of miles to the south, fell in love with the pristine islands the way one falls in love with a person. They composed a whole body of chants and song-poems in honor of the beauty they found, often entwining human passion and love of the land in flowing lyric compositions, such as this verse of the old chant, *Hole Waimea*—

> *Me he ipo la ka maka lena o ke Koolau*
> *Ka pua i ka nahele o Mahuleia*
> *E lei hele i ke alo o Moolau*
> *E lau ka huakai-hele i ka pali loa*
> *Hele hihiu, piliu, noho i ka nahele*
> *O kuu noho wale iho no i kahua, e*
> *A he aloha e*
> *O kou aloha ka i hiki mai i ou nei*
> *Mahea la ia i nalo iho nei?*

> *Dear as my heart Koolau's golden eye*
> *My flower in the forest of Mahuleia,*
> *A wreath of journey to rest on the*
> *   love in my heart,*
> *A welcome shade at the end of my*
> *   long yearning.*
> *Love-touched, weary, mine a*
> *   wilderness home;*
> *I cherish forever the ancient place,*
> *For it is love, indeed.*
> *Your love visits me here.*
> *Where has love been hiding until now?*

The first Hawaiians, realizing the limitations of their island environment, were excellent stewards of the land. Ko Olina is part of the original *moku* of Honouliuli, a royal land division whose boundaries once stretched along the sunniest side of Oahu from the waters of Pearl Harbor to the summit of the Waianae Mountains and west to Nanakuli.

In a uniquely Hawaiian system of resource management, a moku was divided into *ahupuaa*, pie-shaped wedges of land going from the mountain tops to the reefs in the sea. This afforded every family access to different elevations for various crops, and an outlet to the ocean for fishing. The ahupuaa usually incorporated great natural diversity and typically would contain a complete watershed system with running streams, lush rain forest, dry upland forest, mountain slopes, valley, sandy beach and coral reef. Hundreds of

different plants thrived in the varied environment, some cultivated by the Hawaiians, others growing in wild abundance. They included crops such as taro, sweet potato, sugarcane, breadfruit, yam and coconut. Certain shrubs such as noni and olena were grown for medicinal purposes. There were paper mulberry trees whose bark could be pounded into fabric for clothing, giant koa trees to be carved into canoes, and plants to be harvested for tools, weapons, ornaments, cordage, and shelter. Just about everything required for life could be found in the ahupuaa. This holistic system of land stewardship sustained a large population on relatively small isolated islands without the advantages of trade with other places. It also preserved the stunning natural beauty of Hawaii.

When the resort of Ko Olina came to be, this same sense of stewardship, of the sacredness of the land, the sea and the resources, shaped the philosophy of development. The three lovely coves, gifts of Nature, have become seven lagoons. The verdant lawns and greens are showered in plumeria blossoms at the slightest breeze. Coconut palms sway, elegant and drowsy, above sand as white as white orchids. The care of Ko Olina, now as always, is a sacred trust expressed in the words "aloha aina," love of the land. Ko Olina, The Place of Joy, is the song that comes unbidden to the lips, the Paradise we recognize with a knowing beyond knowing.

Pele Creates the Sacred Land

Long, long ago, before there was a need to measure time, Pele-na-wahine-o-Kalua was born as a red flame in the mouth of the great goddess Haumea, mother of mankind. Pele fled from her birthplace in Tahiti to escape the wrath of her jealous older sister.

"Run," cried her sister, Namaka-o-Kahai, ruler of sea and water, who suspected Pele of loving her husband. "Run as fast as you can. See if you can escape me."

Wisely, because sea and water are stronger than fire and flame, Pele said nothing. Instead she took her longest digging stick and boarded a canoe to race away across the waves. Taking the form of a great shark, Pele's older and favorite brother, Ka-moho-alii, led the way.

Beginning far out in the Hawaiian archipelago, Pele searched for a new home for her sacred fire, digging craters as she went. Many times she nearly succeeded, only to have her sister, close upon her heels, fill the crater with the sea.

But Pele-na-wahine-o-Kalua, the woman of the pit, persisted, moving down the chain of islands. She created the islands of Niihau and Kauai. Then she paused long enough to shape two great calderas, first at Waianae and then at Koolau. Slowly, over eons, their cones grew until eventually they broke through to sea level. Finally, Pele joined her two creations together to shape the Island of Oahu.

Pele made Oahu beautiful, leaving a graceful touch here, another there, taking the time to be certain that the sweeping Waianae peaks and high, green Koolau ridges were both visible from Ko Olina.

Perhaps she took a little too much time because when she moved southeast to shape the Island of Maui her sister Namaka-o-Kahai caught up with her. In Hana, Maui, there is a cinder hill called Ka-iwi-o-Pele, the bones of Pele. It marks the spot where Pele lost her mortal self and became the immortal goddess of volcanos.

To this very day the goddess Pele makes her home on the Island of Hawaii where she continues to build and shape the sacred land. In addition to her work on Kilauea volcano, she is busy with Lo-ihi, a small crater rising beneath the surface of the sea south of Hawaii.

Among the stories of Pele's adventures and appearances in Hawaii, one of the best known and best loved is the romance of Hiiaka and Lohiau. For those interested, a compelling version of the romance was recorded by Kamokila Campbell, a descendent of Hawaiian royalty and former owner of the land on which Ko Olina is situated. Originally taped in 1957, it has been digitally remastered as **Kamokila, Legends of Hawaii***, and is available on CD from the Mountain Apple Company in Honolulu. Music for the legends on the CD was composed by Jack de Mello at Lanikuhonua, Kamokila's estate at Ko Olina.*

The red lehua blossom of the high-altitude ohia tree is sacred to Pele, goddess of volcanos.

Ocean

Earth, from space, is a beautiful blue jewel spinning with amazing life in the star-studded black velvet silence of the universe. Its largest geographic feature is the azure Pacific Ocean. If all the land areas of the world were combined, the result would still be only an island in the Pacific.

The ocean surrounds and defines the fiftieth state as it influences no other. It dominates the climate and has shaped the land itself. It created beaches that are the envy of the world, then protected them by building an intricate network of coral reefs. It provides food and recreation, and fuels the state's major industry, tourism. No place on Oahu is more than eleven miles from the Pacific. Its tides are the governing law, bowing only to the moon.

In a yearly show of force, the Pacific in winter rolls ashore at Makaha in thunderous white-haired waves that cause the land to tremble under the impact. Sunlit and sometimes forty feet high, the monster surf is a turmoil of raw power and turquoise luminosity. People come from all over the island to see it, and surf champions from around the world dare to ride it. Amazingly, just down the road at Ko Olina, the Pacific remains its gentle, lake-like self.

Swimming with whales: *a young black pilot whale allows a snorkeler to accompany him for a swim.*

Oahu has more than 150 beaches, and the lagoons of Ko Olina, sheltered, sun-drenched and palm-fringed, are the best swimming beaches of them all. Just ask the experts — rare Hawaiian monk seals still make their way to the sheltered coves to bask in the sun and snooze in undisturbed peace.

The waters around Ko Olina are among the calmest and clearest fronting Oahu, making the sparkling offshore ocean exceptional for diving, fishing, snorkeling and sailing. These

qualities are greatly appreciated not only by the people who come to the sea, but by the denizens of the deep, who live in it. Sizable pods of spinner dolphins, the gymnasts of the sea, call the area home. Some people attribute healing powers to the dolphins, and indeed, research continues into their usefulness in treating neurological diseases, especially in children. Dolphins have the ability to remember, to initiate creative patterns of behavior, and to understand language, both spoken and gestured. Many people travel to the western shores of Oahu to encounter these highly intelligent sea mammals. They report life-changing experiences after swimming with dolphins.

The dolphin or porpoise is a cetacean, the order of marine mammals also containing whales. These animals are warm-blooded, breathe air and suckle their young. The dolphins are, in fact, a variety of Odontoceti, or toothed whales. The other variety of whale is the Mysticeti, or toothless whales. Mysticeti refers to the baleen, the strange comb-like moustache that serves as a feeding mechanism. The whale's "mustache" is so efficient it can trap as much as two tons of plankton, krill and small sea animals in a single feeding.

The humpback whales, which frequent Hawaiian waters, belong to the Mysticeti. Between November and April, the strange haunting song of the humpback whale echoes along the waves as the gentle giants of the deep settle in for a season to mate, give birth to their young and fatten the two-ton babies for the long swim north to the Arctic feeding grounds. Their fantastic gymnastics delight all who see them. They leap, spout and splash as if they are lithe ballerinas and not sixty-foot behemoths weighing over 100,000 pounds each. Humpbacks are the third most endangered species of whale with a world population of only 7,000 to 8,000 individuals. This may be hard to believe when they

congregate in such numbers in Hawaiian waters. State and federal laws prohibit approaching within 300 feet of a whale. The whales, however, observe no such laws and sometimes swim right up to the boats that go out to observe them, giving everyone on board a glimpse of the wildness and immensity of the liquid universe that does not conform itself to notions of borders and limits, but recognizes only survival and freedom.

Black pilot whales are also found in great numbers, traveling in pods of two to three dozen. Other whales in Hawaiian waters are false killer whales, melon-headed whales, beaked whales and even the mighty sperm whale, the whale that inspired the great American novel *Moby Dick* by Herman Melville. As a young seaman, Melville spent time in the Islands gathering grist for his many books. He wrote of the Pacific: "To any meditative...rover, this serene Pacific, once beheld, must ever after be the sea of his adoption. It rolls the midmost waters of the world, the Indian Ocean and the Atlantic being but its arms."

Boats leave Ko Olina Marina daily, taking people out into those wonderful waters to meet our neighbor creatures. Dolphins and flying fish are almost guaranteed. The rest is serendipity.

The endangered Hawaiian monk seal frequents seas between Kauai and Ko Olina.

Dolphin and her newborn calf in Hawaiian waters.

begins its story in the ocean depths, and it names the coral polyp as Earth's first creature. The coral reefs of the Pacific are the most magnificent and diverse in the world. The Caribbean, renowned for its dive sites, has forty-eight kinds of coral, the Pacific more than 600, plus 4,000 species of fish. The vast coral reef that runs from the eastern side of Kalaeloa, past Ko Olina and on to Nanakuli is one of the most extensive in Hawaii. It is also one of the most ancient.

The centuries-old coral colonies of Ko Olina are among the oldest living marine organisms in this part of the Pacific. The coral heads are massive. At Ko Olina the reef runs close to shore and plays host to an extremely varied fish population. This intricate network of coral owes its antiquity to the natural storm protection afforded by the contours of the land. The reef is a natural treasure and it's right at Ko Olina's doorstep.

Hawaii is as beautiful below the sea as above. Since the islands are the tops of marine mountains, a sort of inverted Himalaya, the ocean falls off to great depths quite close to shore. Divers sailing from Ko Olina will discover coral canyons, lava slopes and intricate coral reefs teeming with colorfully spangled fish, the Moorish idol, the parrot fish, the angel fish, and the snouty humuhumunukunukuapuaa. They flit about as swiftly as thoughts, darting among coral convolutions. It is a kaleidoscope of jubilant color blooming in undulating sea blossoms and scattered with crimson sea stars. To swim amidst such beauty and silence is to bear witness to a creation so intense, so delicate, so ancient as to inspire rapture.

Coral reefs are to the ocean what rain forests are to the land. They survived ice ages and rises and drops in sea levels. The *Kumulipo*, the masterpiece Hawaiian chant of creation,

The ocean teams in such an abundance of fish, that Oahu's seafood is always fresh and delectable. Mahimahi, ulua, opakapaka, onaga and opah have become the foundation of Hawaii's now famous regional cuisine. All along the western coast, from Ko Olina to Kaena Point, fishermen still cast their lines and nets to snare the ocean's bounty. At times, the fish have been so plentiful that people on shore reported seeing hundreds of them swimming in the high curl of the waves. Charter fishing boats can be arranged at Ko Olina Marina.

Ko Olina Lagoon Three: Morning at Naia (Dolphin) Lagoon.

The Marina, which opened the year of the Millennium, was the first private boat facility to be constructed in Hawaii in three decades. Until Ko Olina, Hawaii was not taken seriously as a yachting destination.

Ko Olina is sailing in the impressive wake of a long seafaring tradition. The Hawaiians were the lords of the ocean. They were criss-crossing vast reaches of the Pacific before the fall of Troy, while Europeans still clung to sight of land, afraid of falling off the "flat Earth." With the wind, stars and ocean currents as guides, these "Vikings of the Sunrise" colonized the Pacific, sailing from one archipelago to the next across uncharted seas.

They celebrated their exploits in songs and hula, but without a written record, no one believed them. In 1976, the Hawaii-based Polynesian Voyaging Society, using oral history and early sketches of canoes, finished constructing *Hokulea*, a sixty-foot replica of an ancient voyaging canoe. They sailed it to Tahiti and back, proving that such journeys were possible, but not necessarily done. Then in 1981 on the island of Huahine Nui in French Polynesia, workmen excavating for a resort tennis court, discovered the hull of an eighty-five-foot canoe, a twelve-foot steering paddle, and artifacts linking the site with other Polynesian nations. They were more than a thousand years old. Investigation revealed that a tidal wave covered what was then a thriving ship-building center. The wave deposited just the right mixture of sand, salt and silt to protect the objects from the ravages normally inflicted by a tropical climate. Finally, Polynesia yielded its secrets and the ancient songs were proven true.

Hokulea still sails in Hawaiian waters, its distinctive claw-shaped sail perfectly at home on the horizon. The canoe has called at Ko Olina Marina and will always be welcomed. It takes its place proudly beside the luxury yachts and power boats that evolved much later, but sail no truer.

In December 1998 under conditions of utmost secrecy at Ko Olina, construction began on a multi-million-dollar racing yacht to compete in the year 2000 America's Cup, the world's most prestigious sailing competition.

A ninety-six-foot-long oven on wheels was built to cure the sleek carbon fiber hull of *Abracadabra 2000*, and a back-up hull, each measuring eighty feet. When finished, the vessels were tested in waters off Ko Olina, then shipped to New Zealand for the race.

Abracadabra 2000 made a spirited showing and caused the yachting world to take a new look at Hawaii as a serious boating destination. The mission, therefore, was successful.

It was the ocean that kept Hawaii hidden long after most of the world was mapped, and it was the ocean that brought the world to Hawaii's doorstep in 1778 when British Captain James Cook stumbled upon the world's most remote islands.

For the Hawaiians, Cook's arrival was the equivalent of a space ship landing today. Islanders encountered, for the first time, new ships, new races of people, new animals and plants, a new religion and new culture. Unfortunately, they also were exposed to new diseases to which they, living so long in isolation, had no immunities. In less than one hundred years it is estimated that ninety percent of the Hawaiian people died. The survival of the race and culture against such odds can only be attributed to the endurance and spirit of the people, their love of their land and legacy, and miraculous grace.

Sixteen years after Cook's arrival, Captain William Brown aboard the *H.M.S. Jackal,* came upon Honolulu Harbor, which his predecessor had missed. Word quickly spread among traders plying Pacific routes, and the little fishing village with the deep harbor grew into one of the world's great cities, thirty minutes from Ko Olina.

In former times, inter-island travel was by outrigger canoe. Today, these swift ocean-going canoes can be seen along the western coast, as paddlers practice ancient skills to compete in outrigger regattas, turning mere transportation into a highly popular sport.

The first trans-Pacific air flights to Hawaii were by seaplane. In 1925, American pilot John Rodgers and a four-man crew attempted to cross the ocean in a P9N seaplane and ran out of fuel 300 miles from Hawaii. They ripped material from the underside of the wings, rigged sails, and nine days later, right on course, were rescued by a submarine in Hawaiian waters. The first solo flight between Hawaii and the Mainland was made in 1935 by Amelia Earhart in a single-engine Lockheed Vega monoplane. The first commercial airline flight to Hawaii was in 1936 when Pan American's China Clipper seaplane flew from San Francisco to Honolulu in the amazing time of twenty-one hours and thirty-three minutes. Passengers dined on consommé and chicken fricassee served on white linen with wine and silver. After dessert, they retired to their staterooms and the steward shined their shoes and pressed their clothes while they slept. They paid $720 for their round-trip ticket.

The Pacific Ocean can now be crossed to Hawaii in five jet hours, putting the Place of Joy, Ko Olina, just a meal and a movie away from the West Coast of the United States.

Looking at the Pacific from The Place of Joy, it is hard to tell where ocean ends and sky begins. The horizon is limitless.

Surfers from around the world come to the North Shore of Oahu, a short drive from Ko Olina, to ply the world-famous Banzai Pipeline or catch a big one at Waimea Bay, pictured facing page 21. Spectators are welcome during a series of major international surf meets held every winter when the waves and sets are best for this exciting sport practiced in Hawaii since pre-Western times.

The ocean has always been a draw for those who love to travel by sea in Hawaii: at left, the Polynesian voyaging canoe **Hokulea** on a round-the-island sail, circa 1999; above: a Pan American China Clipper seaplane at anchor in an Oahu lagoon circa 1936; right: pleasure boats and yachts at Ko Olina Marina.

How the Reef Fish of Hawaii Got Their Colors

Once, in a time when the world was much newer, a young couple of royal descent lived beside one of the ancient lagoons at Ko Olina, on the island of Oahu. Their marriage was arranged at birth so that children born to them would be of even greater royal lineage. Although they met first on the day of their wedding, afterward they fell deeply in love.

Kekau, the husband, was an expert in the art of fishing. In those days the reef fish of Hawaii had no colors, but they came in many shapes and sizes that Kekau could tell apart. He knew when to direct the village fishermen to launch their outrigger canoes into the deep channel between Oahu and Kauai to catch *ulua*, or jackfish. He could explain the best uses for the five ages of *ama-ama*, or mullet. Because of his skills, the people of Ko Olina always had enough fish to eat.

Kekau's wife, Noelani, knew all about the beautiful birds of Oahu's rain forest. She was an expert at finding those birds whose red, yellow and black feathers were used to make leis and ceremonial capes for the *ali'i*, or royalty. From Noelani the people of Ko Olina learned how beauty uplifts the heart.

One day when Kekau and Noelani had been married for about a year, the high priest arrived at their house. "I have come to oversee the birth of your first child," he declared. "After it is born, I will take it to the royal court on the other side of Oahu to be raised."

"That's too far away," protested Kekau.

"We won't be able to see our child," cried Noelani.

"That is the rule," said the priest. "Your child will be more royal than any other in Hawaii. It must be brought up in the royal court."

That night Kekau and Noelani prayed together to do what was best for the child-to-come. Separately, they prayed to find a way to keep the child closer to them.

The next day Noelani went to the rain forest to see her beloved birds. There she heard the sweet trilling of the yellow-tufted o-o, a bird famous for its beautiful song. The o-o saw tears on Noelani's cheeks. It stopped singing.

"What is the matter, lovely Noelani?" the o-o asked. Noelani poured out her story.

That same day Kekau went to the lagoon where he was raising a breed of ama-ama that could swim from Ko Olina around the island to Laie and back. As he waded into the sea, a school of the slippery fish gathered around him playfully.

"Kekau is not himself," the ama-ama said to one another. "He isn't trying to catch us the way he usually does."

"What's wrong, Kekau?" asked the eldest of the ama-ama. As Kekau told his story other fish swam into the lagoon to hear it. The ama-ama, the manini and lau-ipala, the uhu, kihikihi and the humuhumunukunukuapuaa with its nose shaped like a pig's, all listened.

Later that day Kekau and Noelani both returned home where they did their best to prepare for giving their child away. Soon the time for the birth arrived.

The night before, Kekau had an unusual dream. In it he was counting fish in the lagoon to be sure there would be enough to eat in the coming months. Because the fish were all the same color he kept getting the count wrong. Just as he was about to give up, a beautiful woman clothed in seaweed swam up from the bottom of the lagoon.

"Are you Kekau, the husband of Noelani?" she asked.

"I am," said Kekau, cautiously.

"I am Halelehua, goddess of this sea," the woman said. "Tomorrow when your daughter Keikilani is born, bring her to me. The gods have something important for her to do."

Before he could reply, Kekau woke up. He was on his own sleeping mat. Several pieces of seaweed were caught in his clothes. Noelani was sleeping soundly beside him.

Through a crack in the roof above the young couple, a sunbeam brought the first light of day inside. On it, a yellow feather drifted slowly downward and settled gently on Noelani's nose. She sat up with a start and sneezed. "I had the most amazing dream," she said, rubbing her eyes. "I was in the rain forest and the o-o said that we would have a daughter named Keikilani and that we should give her to Halelehua, the sea goddess who lives in our lagoon."

"You dreamed the same thing I did," Kekau said, astonished.

Kekau and Noelani asked the priest to explain the meaning of their dreams. After listening carefully, he said, "This means that you should allow your daughter to be adopted by Halelehua. The gods have a special plan for your child."

Keikilani, which means child of heaven, came into the world the next morning. Noelani and Kekau wrapped her in a new piece of white *kapa*, or bark cloth. Then they carried her to the lagoon. A gentle rain was falling. In the distance, a glorious rainbow arched across the Waianae Mountains. It fell onto the lagoon, bathing it in different colors.

"Halelehua," Kekau called, wading into the water. "Here is Keikilani." When the sea goddess appeared, Kekau placed his daughter in her outstretched arms. Noelani took the feather lei she always wore from her own head and placed it on Halelehua's.

"Thank you," said Halelehua, as she gazed fondly at Keikilani. All the fish in the lagoon swam over to greet the new child.

As the young couple turned away to leave, Halelehua called out to them, "Kekau and Noelani, watch for the *po makole*, the night rainbow. When next it appears come again to the lagoon. Your daughter will have something to show you."

Many seasons passed without a rainbow ever shining at night in the Waianae skies. Then, late in the day on the fourth anniversary of Keikilani's birth, a heavy mist gathered against the mountains. That night, after the moon rose, the circle of color that is the rare night rainbow appeared. As soon as they saw it, Kekau and Noelani hurried to the lagoon. Drawing near, they heard happy laughter. A beautiful little girl was standing in the shallows, bathed in moonlight and color. In her small hands were many brightly colored feathers. As Kekau and Noelani watched, two gray fish bounced up to her, a lau-ipila and an uhu.

"It's my turn. Paint me. Paint me!" said the lau-ipala. Keikilani touched the fish's round body and high fins with a yellow feather. Warm shades of golden yellow spread across the little fish.

"Don't I look wonderful?" the lau-ipala said, as it danced away in the lagoon.

Next, the uhu shouldered its way through other gathering fish to Keikilani. "Do me next. Do me. You promised."

Rows of feathers were lined up on the sand next to Keikilani like paints on an artist's palette. The young artist chose carefully for the uhu, first some yellow feathers and then a few blue ones. Before long the fat fish was painted in a pleasing pattern of blue, yellow and green. It swam away smugly.

Kekau and Noelani spent that night and all the next day watching their daughter paint the reef fish of Hawaii in beautiful colors. She put dots of red and white on some; others she left gray but added stripes of black and white. When her creations swam away, the sea glittered with color.

Through the years, Kekau and Noelani returned to the lagoon often. Kekau found more fish that needed coloring and brought them to Keikilani. Noelani brought new feathers from her gathering trips in the rain forest. The parents never tired of watching their daughter at work. Although they missed being able to take her home with them, it was because of their unselfish love that the reef fish of Hawaii became works of art.

Yesterday

For as long as anyone can remember, Ko Olina has been a place of joy. Before the written word, the virtues of this sunny, divinely blessed area of Oahu were told from one generation to the next. Hawaiian nobility once sojourned here when weary of the cares of state. The royal chiefs, their wives, children and retinues came to fish in the bountiful waters, race their outrigger canoes and celebrate life in their island paradise. The children played safely in the calm waters and on the golden sands, listening to the rhythmic tap-tapping of *kapa* beaters, as their mothers pounded tree bark into strong light fabric for clothing and bedding.

The young men practiced martial arts, such as the highly refined discipline known as *lua*, to test their prowess and be ready to defend with their lives and honor all that they beheld of joy and bounty in the scene before them. Old men amused themselves with *ulu maika*, a form of bowling using rounded lava rocks for balls.

The songs of birds filled the air in the early morning when the *kia manu*, the bird catchers, would be about their work, collecting plumage for the magnificent feather capes and helmets required by the chiefs. They plucked the choice feathers and released the birds to flap away to freedom while children clapped in delight.

The people of the *ahupuaa*, the land section that stretched from mountain to sea, brought gifts of taro from the lowlands, *opae* (shrimp) from the streams, milk from the coconut, and kukui nuts, sweet potato and banana from the uplands. From the fisheries at Puuloa, now known as Pearl Harbor, and the great aquaculture pond of Laulaunui came mullet, awa, crab, and oysters. From the ocean came mahimahi, opakapaka and the *opihi*, the limpet that clings to the rocks where the surf breaks. Succulent pigs were steamed in the *imu*, the earthen oven lined in lava rocks. Kava was brewed, and sugarcane cut for treats. Then in the cool of the ocean breezes at the shoreline at Ko Olina the luau feasts would begin and last for days. Dancers draped in kapa and adorned in palapalae ferns would step upon the hula mound and tell with their hands and feet and voices the stories of Hawaii, the explorations, adventures, royal love affairs, and the genealogies of the kings.

In the old stories, the caretaker of Ko Olina was a priest named Napuaikamao. It was his responsibility to maintain this Place of Joy, which in the sixteenth century was the favorite retreat of High Chief Kakuhihewa when he wanted to get away from the busyness of Waikiki. It is said that Kakuhihewa planted ten thousand coconut trees on Oahu. Undoubtedly, he planted some at Ko Olina. Some of the tall palm trees gracing the resort today may be their descendants.

In later years, Queen Kaahumanu, wife of Kamehameha the Great, the king who united all the Hawaiian Islands into one nation, and Queen Liliuokalani, Hawaii's last reigning monarch, traveled to Ko Olina to rest and refresh their spirits in the exceptionably beautiful setting.

The ahupuaa of Honouliuli, in which Ko Olina is situated, was the largest land unit on the island of Oahu. Instead of one gorge, it had five: Awanui, Palailai, Makaiwa, Waimanalo, and Lumaloa. Twelve miles of sun-drenched shoreline ruffled in coves and ponds added to its desirability. Kamapuaa, one of the great gods of the Hawaiian pantheon, was said to have made his home within the ahupuaa at Puu Kapolei, where he lived with his grandmother Kamaunuahihio. There was once a temple at the spot.

At the time of the Great Mahele of 1848, when Hawaiian land was, for the first time, allowed to pass from the ownership of the chiefs to the people, the choice lands of the ahupuaa of Honouliuli, including the fabled place of joy, Ko Olina, were claimed by Miriam Keahi-Kuni Kekauonohi, a granddaughter of Kamehameha the Great. She was a chiefess so *kapu* (sacred) that all other chiefesses had to uncover themselves and lay prostrate in her presence. As a child, Kekauonohi would sit on the chest of her grandfather, the hero king, and merrily tease his thoughtfulness into laughter.

The complicated romances of Hawaiian royalty rivaled the marital convolutions of European dynasties and in the course of her life, Kekauonohi first married Lunalilo, King Kamehameha II. After his death, she lived with her half-brother who was governor of Kauai, then ran away with a stepson of her stepmother Queen Kaahumanu, and finally settled down to marry Chief Levi Haalelea. When Kekauonohi died in 1851, her husband inherited her land. Upon his death, the property passed to his surviving wife who leased it in 1871 to James Dowsett and John Meek for ranching.

In 1877, James Campbell purchased most of the Honouliuli ahupuaa for $95,000. Campbell was one of the colorful characters who arrived in Hawaii in the nineteenth century and stayed to shape the destiny of

the fledgling kingdom. Born February 4, 1826, in Derry, Ireland, his parents were William and Martha (Adams) Campbell. William was of the Campbell clan of Inverary, Scotland, and was a carpenter with a struggling cabinetry business. Because James was not the eldest son, his prospects were limited, so he left home at the age of thirteen to seek his fortune. He stowed away on a schooner bound for Canada, then made his way to New York where he worked in his father's profession as a carpenter. Two years later, only fifteen years old, he shipped out on a Yankee whaler headed for the Pacific. He never saw action. The ship ran aground on a reef in the Tuamotu Islands.

James and two shipmates survived by clinging to a spar and floating ashore to a nearby island. The local inhabitants seized them and tied them to coconut trees while they discussed their fate. The quick-witted James, noticing that the chief was holding a broken musket, indicated he could fix it. When he did, the three castaways were released and welcomed into the island community. James escaped a few months later by swimming out and climbing aboard a passing schooner bound for Tahiti.

He ended up in Hawaii in 1850 aboard a whaler that called at Lahaina, Maui. He got one look at the Hawaiian Islands and his adventuring days were over. He settled into work as a carpenter, boarded with a European family and married their only daughter, Hannah Barla. She left him a childless widower in 1858. While still grieving, he was asked by an acquaintance, John Maipinepine, to build a wooden cradle for the man's infant daughter, Abigail. He never dreamed that nineteen years later, baby Abigail would become his second wife.

With property he had inherited from the Barlas, and his own savings, James and two partners established the Pioneer Mill Company to process the sugarcane thriving on Maui plantations. In the early stages, James, accustomed to hard work, labored beside his workers in the sugar fields and the mill. Pioneer Mill grew so profitable, James became known as "Kimo Ona-Milliona" (James the Millionaire).

He married Abigail Kuaihelani Maipinepine, now a beautiful young woman, on October 30, 1877, sold his interest in the Pioneer Mill Company and moved to Honolulu. The Campbells entertained lavishly in their home on Emma Street, where Hawaii's beloved Princess Kaiulani had been born. Two of the Campbells' own daughters, Alice Kamokila and Muriel Kuahielaniahumanu, were born there. When James wanted to escape from the demands of business and the tumult of daughters, he would retreat to a little aerie on the roof of his house and draw up the ladder so no one could follow.

The Campbells invested heavily in land on Oahu, including the large parcel at Honouliuli. To provide water to the dry, sun-drenched lands, he brought in a California well-driller who went down 240 feet and found water so pure the Hawaiians called the kingdom's first artesian well "Wai-Aniani," crystal waters. Campbell went on to sink seventy-one more wells, transforming his arid leeward fiefdom into prime agricultural ground.

In 1889, James leased part of his holdings to Benjamin Franklin Dillingham, who in turn sub-leased it to sugar growers. Dillingham also operated a feedlot on the Honouliuli land, to fatten Neighbor Island cattle shipped by barge to the market in Honolulu. His most innovative enterprise was the laying of track for the Oahu Railway & Land Company in 1890. It hauled sugarcane, livestock, freight and passengers from Honolulu around Kaena Point to Haleiwa. Passengers from the city rode the train to enjoy the island's leeward and north shore beaches and stay at the Dowsett Hotel at Keaupuni Point, behind where the Waianae Fire Station stands today, and at the Haleiwa Hotel in Haleiwa town.

There was not a businessman on Oahu who thought the plantation train would work, and over drinks at their clubs, they called it "Dillingham's Folly."

Much later, on December 7, 1941, when Japan bombed Pearl Harbor, the little railroad was pressed into service and its 600 employees mobilized to evacuate families out of the Pearl Harbor area and carry in repair and rescue crews. Materials and

Abigail Kuaihelani Maipinepine Campbell and children.

Unlike Dillingham, James Campbell's every business move was watched with a mixture of admiration and envy for he seemed to succeed at everything he touched. Serano Bishop, a neighbor of many years, and the editor of *The Friend,* wrote of him: "Mr. Campbell was a good citizen, although not a religious man. He was remarkable for sound business courage, qualities very commonly accompanying Scotch descent."

As busy as he was managing his many interests, James served in the House of Nobles of the Hawaiian legislature. At the time of the overthrow of the Hawaiian monarchy in 1893, Campbell was a vocal defender of Queen Liliuokalani and never wavered in his allegiance to her.

In 1896, on a business trip to San Francisco when he was seventy years old, Kimo Ona-Milliona was kidnaped and held for a ransom of $20,000. Though he was terrorized, beaten, and denied food and water for two days, he refused to sign a draft for the money. His weary captors finally released him. When he died at home four years later, the man who had left Ireland penniless at age thirteen, bequeathed an estate valued then at over three million dollars, which has grown into one of the largest trusts in Hawaii. He attributed his accumulated wealth to the principle of always living on less than he

medical supplies were chugged to the disaster scene as fast as they could be assembled. Under armed guard with fixed bayonets a trainload of dynamite was carried from the battle scene in case of a return raid. The only trouble was, no one knew what to do with the explosives, so for three months the "dynamite train" sat on a spur of track in the midst of a sugarcane field.

Ko Olina remained a sanctuary during the war. It was so popular among military officers as a place of rest and rejuvenation they called it fondly, "Camp Bell."

Hawaii's railroad fell into decline after the war as the hauling of freight was taken over by truckers. The remaining twelve miles of O.R.& L. track is now in the custody of the Hawaiian Railway Society and is on the National Register of Historic Places. The society operates a working diesel engine and flatcar on the track, which runs through Ko Olina.

made. In his will he set up a trust, The Estate of James Campbell, naming his beloved Abigail as one of the first trustees. Included in the estate was the prime land at Ko Olina. Abigail later married Colonel Sam Parker.

When she died in 1908, the *Honolulu Advertiser* said that she "was a woman of kind impulses and her gifts aided many persons and institutions. She was generous in a quiet way and her benefactions have served to keep aged Hawaiians and people who have seen better days, in comfort."

James Campbell left it to The Estate to implement the vision of his Place of Joy becoming a new population center, a second Honolulu with homes, offices and recreation centers. In 1990, ground was broken for the city of Kapolei, a completely

planned community that has provided for people in all the stages of life. It features residential communities, a government center, medical facilities, schools, churches, temples, childcare centers and homes for the aged and infirm. Its highly sophisticated system of fiber optic and satellite networks has positioned Kapolei in the global electronic market. Hundreds of businesses and tens of thousands of people have been drawn to this manicured city of the future. Parks and recreation were a cornerstone of the vision.

Kamokila, one of the four surviving Campbell daughters, became steward of Lanikuhonua, the sacred area of Ko Olina with its coconut grove, the reef, the coves and the ponds. Kamokila, named for a demi-goddess of ancient Hawaii, earned a reputation every bit as colorful as her

father's. Proud inheritor of two cultures, she was a deeply spiritual person, whose Hawaiian heritage resonated throughout her being. She drew strength from the beauty and *mana*, (power), of Lanikuhonua. Kamokila was a storyteller of great renown, and an enthusiastic supporter of hula in all its forms. Many hula *halau* (schools) still come to Lanikuhonua for retreat and to dance on the old mound. The beat of the *hula pahu* (drum) still resounds along the shores of Ko Olina as it did in ancient times.

With reverence for the site and respect for the Hawaiian tradition of *aloha aina*, love of the land, plans for a 642-acre resort and residential development began to materialize in the 1970s.

Ground was broken for Ko Olina Resort in December 1986.

Pueo, Kulia, and the Ki Ponds of Ko Olina

Kulia and his aging grandfather Kona-pili-ahi grew ki (ti) plants in the brackish water of small coral pools along the coast near Ko Olina. Their considerable skill was known far and wide. People walked for days to gather up the silken green and red leaves to use for house thatching, raincapes and sandals or as wrappings for fish and pig cooked in the *imu*, the ground oven. When the great Oahu chief Kakuhihewa came to vacation at Ko Olina, Kulia and Kona-pili-ahi harvested ki leaves to rethatch his house.

The *aumakua*, or family guardian, of Kulia and his grandfather, was *Pueo*, the owl, who always warned them if someone was planning to take something for nothing or was out of favor with the chief where they lived. Pueo also kept the ponds and their small stores of food free of rats by chasing them away.

Kulia and his grandfather ate well because the people who came for ki always brought something in exchange, like red *ohelo* berries and bananas from the uplands, or mullet and other fat fish from the stone-rimmed storage ponds at Pearl Harbor. All year 'round, there were different kinds of seaweeds to harvest and eat, too.

Whatever fish or meat Kulia and Kona-pili-ahi had was shared with Pueo. The owl's meal was set out first, before they dined themselves. Pueo always thanked them politely. "This fish is delicious," he would say, or "I love roast pig!"

Then a time came when no one brought new food to exchange for ki for many days. Kulia was hungry. Kona-pili-ahi grew restless. At night he tossed and turned on his sleeping mat. By day he moved slowly.

One evening before the shade of night had completely blocked the sun, Kona-pili-ahi said to Kulia, "Soon you will be in charge of the ki beds. Before that time comes, I want to plant a bed of *kalo* (taro). After it ripens, I will make poi from it, the poi of my childhood. Then you will become caretaker of the ki plants."

"But grandfather," said Kulia. "We can't plant kalo here. There is no fresh water."

Kona-pili-ahi pointed to the hill that rose behind them, where clumps of clinging *pili* grass and tangled underbrush grew around dark rocks and boulders. "Over there," he said, "you'll find a fresh water spring. My father took me to drink from it when I was a child. We planted our kalo next to it. You and I will plant again

with roots that are still there. First you must find the spring. Then come and get me."

Kulia knew there was no point in protesting. Once his grandfather had spoken, the task must be done.

"I'll go with you," said Pueo, early the next morning. He had just finished eating the tiny piece of fish and two dried ohelo berries Kulia had set out for him. "Maybe I'll find a nice rat to eat!" he said.

"Wait," said Kona-pili-ahi just as Kulia and Pueo were about to leave. "There is one more thing. You must come for me by the ninth night of the moon. The kalo must be planted on the tenth night."

From rock to rock Kulia climbed and Pueo flew, that day and the next, and the next, and the next. Kulia carried a digging stick which he used as a staff to help him climb. He poked it in the ground to see if it came up wet. He took deep breaths to see if he could smell water. He turned over rocks to see if they were wet underneath. Instead of going right to sleep when the sun started going down the way Pueo did, he used the last light of day to scan the landscape for signs of the green growth that meant water was near. He found nothing.

All too soon first light dawned on the ninth day. Kulia was too worried to sleep any more, although Pueo tucked his head under a wing and refused to budge.

"If you're not coming, I'll go by myself," Kulia said to Pueo.

"Oh, all right. Follow me. I know where the spring is," Pueo said.

With that, Pueo flew a few feet to a place where several flat rocks were piled one on top of the other. "Turn these over and you'll find the spring," he said.

Kulia removed the slabs of rock. When he lifted the last one, fresh water gushed from a small rock-lined well and began to cover the ground around them. "We found it! We found it!" he shouted, and ran to the coast to get his grandfather.

When Kulia returned with Kona-pili-ahi, the moon was almost full. Overjoyed, Kona-pili-ahi dug into the ground around the spring and pulled up a root. "Look, here's kalo, sleeping, waiting for me."

Kulia helped Kona-pili-ahi replant the kalo root. Each day for several months he and his grandfather returned to the spring to work the ground around it until it was time to harvest the kalo.

Finally, an evening came when Kulia and Kona-pili-ahi were sitting on the beach at sunset. Earlier that day Kulia had helped his grandfather pound a new kalo root into fresh poi. They were going to eat it with some fish received in exchange for ki that day. When Pueo flew over to join them, Kulia held up one finger with a scoop of poi on it for him.

"Eeeyu. . .no thank you," said Pueo. "I prefer fish or pig."

Kulia took the next moment to ask about something that had been bothering him. "Pueo," he said, offering the owl a choice piece of freshly caught mullet and popping the fingerful of poi into his own mouth, "if you knew where the spring was all the time, why didn't you take me to it on the first day?"

"'*Umi 'ia i nui keaho*,'" said Pueo, sharing an old proverb. "You needed to 'press hard and take a long breath'," the owl explained. "It takes patience and perseverence to become caretaker of the Ko Olina ki ponds."

With plenty of fish and poi to eat and not so much work to do, Kona-pili-ahi lived to a ripe old age. Kulia remained caretaker of the ki ponds of Ko Olina until his own grandson was ready to take over. For more years than can be counted Pueo and his children, grandchildren, great-grandchildren and great-great-grandchildren kept guard over them all.

People

A journey is at the root of everyone's Hawaiian story, and at the heart of every journey is a quest. Sometimes what's sought is unspoken or even unrecognized at the outset. It might be an idea as lofty as freedom, as basic as survival or as frivolous as fun. Some people plan to spend forever in the Islands, to have their bones rest beneath the mid-ocean mountains or their ashes someday ride the long waves. Many come for a while, a few seasons of life, then move on to greener pastures, more familiar rhythms. Most people jet in on holiday, wish they could stay and vow to return.

Every outward journey has its inner parallel journey. And it is here, in the realm of the spirit, that all who are drawn to Hawaii's shores find a common home of the heart. This is due not only to the incredible natural beauty of the place, and a definite spiritual force that is almost tangible, but to the power of aloha, the philosophy of life planted here by Hawaii's first people, the Polynesians.

Sailing north from the Marquesas Islands, these intrepid explorers found Hawaii almost two thousand years ago. A later wave of settlers arrived from Tahiti between

Four friends at a Japanese Festival.

A.D. 500 and 750. The accepted date for the settlement of Oahu is A.D. 600, although new archeological evidence may push that date earlier in time. Those first Hawaiians, sailed with their gods on the twin bows of their great voyaging canoes and brought with them the plants and animals they deemed necessary for life.

It is difficult to imagine following stars where no one else had gone before, not knowing what, if anything, would be found, and discovering in the middle of the sea, such beautiful uninhabited islands, green, fertile, forested, and flowing with water. The weary sailors knew they had found a

Place of Joy. In Hawaii, the Polynesian culture enjoyed its greatest flowering.

There is lively speculation as to who arrived next. Captain Cook gets the credit, but there is some evidence that the Manila galleons of Spain may have gotten here two hundred years earlier. There are old stories of seven white-skinned castaways who landed at Kealakekua Bay on the Big Island. Immediately upon touching shore, they knelt in prayer. The Hawaiians, alert to matters of the spirit, welcomed them, and according to oral history, the men stayed and married into chiefly families. Pedro Ordonez de Ceballos wrote of landing in

1589 at islands that he described in the neighborhood of Hawaii and encountering Spanish-speaking descendants of a shipwreck. Several old Spanish maps show islands labeled "Las Mesas" positioned at the same latitude as Hawaii. One of these jealously guarded charts fell into the hands of the British. Captain Cook carried a copy of the captured map on his voyage of exploration of the Pacific. Cook reported that the Hawaiians had knowledge of iron, and possessed several pieces of metal even though there was none naturally in their environment.

In the wake of Cook's discovery, a raft of American and European adventurers poured into the islands, first in a trickle, then a deluge. The Yankee Pacific whaling fleet began calling in Hawaiian ports in 1819. Hot on their heels, breathing fire and brimstone, came the New England missionaries. The latter group influenced every aspect of Hawaiian life. They brought a new faith to a deeply spiritual people who had overthrown their own religion only the year before. The missionaries transliterated the Hawaiian language, established the first schools west of the Rocky Mountains and brought Western melodic concepts to Island music. Those first songs combining Hawaiian and Western traditions were *himeni*, hymns. The melodious himeni can still be heard in the little churches of many denominations all along the Waianae Coast.

The Americans knew opportunity when they saw it, and quickly established vast sugar and pineapple plantations, which necessitated importing a large supply of cheap labor. The first workers they recruited came from China. While Chinese crewmen serving aboard British vessels began arriving in 1788, the first big immigration began in 1852 when 293 Chinese men stepped ashore with five-year contracts to work on the sugar plantations. Wages were three dollars a month. As soon as the Chinese workers fulfilled their contracts, they left the plantations and started small businesses. Within ten years of their arrival, the Chinese operated sixty percent of the wholesale and retail business in the Islands. They had a saying, "Lucky come Hawaii."

Honolulu's Chinatown, on the fringes of the downtown financial district, is, today, the largest historical district in the state. A half-hour's drive from Ko Olina, it is known for its many art and antique galleries, open markets, lei shops, importers, restaurants, and walking tours.

The first Japanese, like the first Spanish, are thought to have arrived as shipwrecked castaways, although there is no

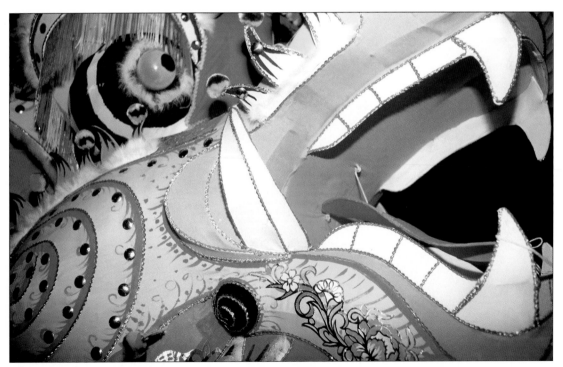

A raucous Lion Dance held at propitious moments helps ensure good fortune for Chinese enterprises and family celebrations in the Islands.

documentation for this. Approximately 150 men and women arrived in 1868 as plantation laborers from Yokohama. The real wave of Japanese immigration, however, began in 1885 when 900 workers arrived in "Golden Hawaii" aboard the *City of Tokio*. By 1924, the Japanese numbered more than forty percent of the population, the largest ethnic group in the Islands. In World War II, the Japanese-American military contingent, the 442nd Regimental Combat Team, served with outstanding valor in the European theater, and became the most decorated unit in the United States Army. Returning veterans, armed with the G.I. Bill, sought higher education, and emerged as a major political force in Hawaii, even electing the nation's first Asian-American governor, George Ariyoshi, in 1974. One of the most exquisite examples of Japanese culture in the Islands is the Byodo-In Temple set against the Koolau Mountains of Windward Oahu. During *Bon Odori* season from June through August, Japanese temples on all islands are swagged in paper lanterns, the taiko drums boom and everyone, regardless of ethnicity, is invited to join the *bon* dancing, and float lanterns out to sea, honoring ancestors.

The first recorded Portuguese settler in Hawaii is Joao Elliot de Castro. He served as secretary and advisor to King Kamehameha the Great. During the whaling era, ships from the Portuguese islands of Madeira and the Azores called in Hawaiian ports and suffered great losses of crew as the men, recognizing a place of joy when they saw one, jumped ship to stay. The ship *Priscilla* carried one hundred eighty Portuguese men, women and

children to the Islands in 1878, the first in a wave of thousands of immigrants. One of the new arrivals, Manuel Nunes, brought with him a Madeiran musical instrument called the braguinha, which became Hawaii's beloved ukulele.

Other significant immigrations have come from Korea, Puerto Rico and Samoa, and, of course, the American Mainland. People are still arriving from all points of the compass. They come as professionals, laborers and surfers who wait tables at night so they can ride the waves all day. With a little effort, the *malihini*, newcomers, quickly weave themselves into the diverse tapestry of Island life, celebrating each other's holidays and traditions, marking on their calendars: Christmas, Cherry Blossom Festival, Chinese New Year, Kamehameha Day and the Fourth of July. They fall in love and marry across racial lines at a rate that hovers around fifty percent. Their children are a happy golden blend, a new irresistibly appealing race who proudly call themselves, "chop suey." The faces of Ko Olina represent the combined heritages of the world's many honored cultures.

All this is possible because of the generosity and the precedent set by the first Hawaiians. Their philosophy of aloha, of welcoming the stranger, is the cornerstone of Island life. *Alo* means "in the presence of" and *ha* is the breath of life, God. When we say, "Aloha," we are recognizing that we stand together in the presence of God and so we need to treat each other with respect and love. Aloha is the spirit of the Place of Joy, Ko Olina.

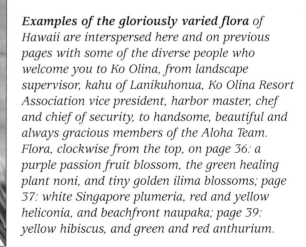

Examples of the gloriously varied flora of Hawaii are interspersed here and on previous pages with some of the diverse people who welcome you to Ko Olina, from landscape supervisor, kahu of Lanikuhonua, Ko Olina Resort Association vice president, harbor master, chef and chief of security, to handsome, beautiful and always gracious members of the Aloha Team. Flora, clockwise from the top, on page 36: a purple passion fruit blossom, the green healing plant noni, and tiny golden ilima blossoms; page 37: white Singapore plumeria, red and yellow heliconia, and beachfront naupaka; page 39: yellow hibiscus, and green and red anthurium.

The Water Lizard and the Pearl Oysters

Once upon a time not so long ago, there were many pearl oysters in the sea ponds of Pearl Harbor. The pearls they grew shone with the reflected colors of the rainbow.

Kanekua-ana, a Hawaiian *mo-o*, or water lizard, brought the pearl oysters from Tahiti. A great and benevolent mo-o, she was the *aumakua*, or guardian spirit, of the shellfish of Pearl Harbor.

The people who lived in the village nearby built a special temple where they left pigs, bananas and coconuts for Kanekua-ana. In return, she filled the sea ponds with tasty mussels, limpets, shrimp, and anchovies. The fat and delicious pearl oysters she also left were the villagers' favorite food.

The Hawaiians of old were very wise fishermen. They had many methods of being sure there would always be enough food. So that all the shellfish might multiply and increase, collecting them was *kapu*, or forbidden, at certain seasons. Hau tree branches were placed on the shoreline to show that it was the kapu season.

One day while the kapu was in place, an elderly widow walked down to the sea ponds from her home in the uplands. She carried a basket for the *limu*, or

seaweed, she planned to take home. When she arrived, she was surprised to see dozens of pearl oysters on the rocks in the shallows. "What beautiful oysters!" she said.

The old widow was the first of the day's seaweed gatherers to reach the ponds. No one else was around. Since she hadn't eaten fish for many days, she leaned down and picked just enough of the oysters for herself and put them in the bottom of her basket. Then she walked along the shore and gathered seaweed. She put it into the basket on top of the oysters.

When the old widow was finished and was getting ready to go home, the headman of the area appeared. "This looks too heavy for seaweed," he said, taking her basket and turning it upside down. Its contents fell into one of the ponds, seaweed, oysters and all. "You've broken the kapu, old woman," he said. "You must pay my fine."

"Please," the old woman said, "I am a poor widow who has no one to fish for her. Now my seaweed is gone with the oysters. Tonight I will not eat." She started slowly up the path toward her home, with the headman following her. "That's no concern of mine," he said. "Pay me."

When the old widow could stand his pestering no longer, she reached into a pocket in her muumuu for a coin given to her by one of the new foreigners who had come from over the ocean to live in her land. "Here, take this. It's all I have."

Taking the coin, the headman said, "Good. Now go." He turned away rudely to see what more he could get from the seaweed gatherers still at the ponds.

Kanekua-ana had been watching all this from beneath the sea. It made her very angry. She was fond of the old widow who always followed the old ways and left offerings for her at the temple.

"That headman has been greedy for the last time," Kanekua-ana said to herself. "It's one thing to return the oysters to the sea because of the kapu. It's another to take an old widow's last coin. Besides, where were the other people to defend her? They don't deserve the oysters they like so much!"

That night Kanekua-ana found someone to speak for her to the people. Through him she told the villagers that she was returning to Tahiti with the oysters. She would leave a few, but there would never be so many pearl oysters in Pearl Harbor again.

Today

In the oddly prophetic way of Hawaiian names, the ancient name Ko Olina, meaning Place of Joy, is in the process of being fulfilled on a scale unimagined even by the kings and queens who celebrated its virtues. Located on the driest, sunniest side of Oahu, perfect for enjoying the beauty of the surroundings, Ko Olina lives out its old name, as it has without interruption for centuries.

Today, green open spaces, quiet coves, protected lagoons, golden sands, uninhabited mountain backdrop and a very comfortable lifestyle, can't help but elicit joy in the most urban weary soul. The thousand acres of Ko Olina Resort & Marina have all the virtues of a sanctuary, and all the amenities of a world-class resort. Ko Olina is almost an island within an island, a destination unto itself. And yet it is only twenty minutes from Honolulu International Airport, thirty minutes to the business towers, shops and restaurants of Honolulu, and ten more minutes to Waikiki. The manicured city of Kapolei, Oahu's "second city," with its shops and restaurants, is a mere five minutes from the gates of Ko Olina.

All the action of a major metropolis and the attractions of the world's most popular beach may swirl nearby, but Ko Olina remains a place apart, a place of serenity and joy, bordered by ocean, mountains and the manicured hills and waterways of the Ko Olina Golf Club.

Before anything else, the golf course was built. Ko Olina has always had its priorities straight, and first comes pleasure. Famed golf course designer and player, Ted Robinson, known for his talent in rendering aquatic features, planned the eighteen-hole championship course with sixteen outstanding water features, including ponds, waterfalls and meandering streams. The course's signature eighteenth hole encompasses seven pools, a large lake, and a waterfall among its lovely distractions. Rare black swans glide about imperiously, ignoring the many other species of Hawaiian birds that grace the course with their plumage and song. Hundreds of snow-white Singapore plumeria trees ritually shower the course with their delicate petals. The rounded knolls, splashing water, the views, the birds and flowers all conspire to produce a beautifully cadenced game.

It's no wonder the par-seventy-two layout has hosted such golf events as the LPGA Ladies Hawaiian Open and the Ko Olina Senior PGA Invitational tournaments.

The Golf Club also consists of an award-winning golf shop featuring the famous "lady bug" logo, lockers, showers, Jacuzzi, steam room and the popular Niblick restaurant. State-of-technology equipment enables golfers to plot their moves, keep track of scores and order food and beverage while still playing the course. Global imaging techniques track their progress around the links and aid in navigating the terrain. Professional instruction is available and there is a comprehensive junior program to encourage both visiting and local youths.

If having such a truly great golf facility on property only increases the appetite for the sport, there are a dozen other courses within ten miles of Ko Olina. In fact, this end of the island has been called, by an act of the state legislature, the "Golf Capital of Oahu."

The resort's other major recreational facility is the forty-three-acre Ko Olina Marina. Notched into Kalaeloa Harbor, it is perfectly sheltered from the ocean, and gated for utmost privacy. The resort marina, built at a cost of fifty million dollars and opened in March 2000, was designed in response to a need expressed by the world yachting community for facilities in Hawaii that can handle large luxury vessels. Consequently, the Ko Olina Marina offers 270 slips and can accommodate boats up to 150 feet in length.

Boaters will find all the services they need, including fuel, computer ports, cable television hookups, barbeque and picnic areas, and the General Store. Dolphin excursions, whale watching expeditions, snorkel and dive trips, and charter fishing can be arranged at the Marina.

***The fifty-million-dollar Ko Olina Marina** offers 270 slips and all the attendant facilities for everything from small family cabin cruisers to ocean-going luxury vessels up to 150 feet long. Resort guests and residents may take advantage of whale-watching expeditions, dolphin excursions, snorkel and dive trips, charter fishing and other sea-going adventures offered at the marina.*

***The dramatic Ko Olina Ocean Club** at right, is a popular gathering spot for private events by the sea.*

It is natural that a Place of Joy has a wedding chapel. Crowning the cove at Kohola, Lagoon One, the Ko Olina Wedding Chapel is a romantic gem. Inspired by the facets of a diamond engagement ring, its glass walls look out on exalted panoramic views of the ocean, the sands and the resort. Flurries of white organza billow about on the lawn in the shade of waving palm trees as brides and grooms embrace for wedding photographs that will capture forever the happiness of the moment and the glory of the lagoon-side setting. The chapel's wedding coordinators can handle all the details of large and small weddings, from flowers, limousine service, rental or purchase of gowns and groom attire, minister, champagne—everything except a spouse. There is an additional wedding chapel at Paradise Cove and weddings have also been arranged at the dramatic glass-enclosed Ko Olina Ocean Club.

Romance permeates the air in Hawaii and nowhere more so than at Ko Olina with its extraordinary settings for weddings and celebratory events of all kinds. Above, the glittering Ko Olina Wedding Chapel.

At right, guests cheer "the kiss" *at a wedding held at Ihilani Resort.*

Great celebrations are held every evening at Paradise Cove, Ko Olina, where hundreds of guests gather for Hawaii's biggest luau. The eerie notes of the conch shell call revelers to the feast while hula drums summon the dancers, as they have for centuries. It's as if a window of time has opened and the legendary Hawaii of old again reigns at Ko Olina. In the ambient glow of the setting sun, as it burnishes the sky in gold, tangerine and even green, the ancient Hawaiian pageantry unfolds. Latter-day kings in traditional capes and helmets lead a procession of regally costumed nobility to the ceremonial unearthing of the pig from its *imu*, underground oven. Tables are laden with tropical fruit and the specialties of earth and sea. On stage, a Polynesian extravaganza erupts in fire dancing, hip-swiveling Tahitian *tamurae* and the fluid graceful hula, still telling Hawaii's stories. Guests head home beneath a sky wild with stars.

Visiting Ko Olina can be one of the most rewarding experiences of a lifetime. The JW Marriott Ihilani Resort and Spa at Ko Olina has consistently been voted into the top ranks of the world's spa resorts by leading travel magazines. The celebrated hotel, which has won the coveted AAA Four-Diamond Award, hugs an arm of Kohola Lagoon with views up and down the dramatic Waianae coastline. Among the hotel's offerings are five distinctive restaurants and lounges featuring Hawaii regional cuisine, shopping boutiques, state-of-the-art meeting facilities, a tennis club, and a licensed year-round children's program where education and fun in joyful surroundings awaken children to new possibilities and larger horizons. The hotel's acclaimed spa continues the restorative traditions that once drew royalty to the saltwater ponds still clinging to the shore. European, Asian and Hawaiian treatments include a specialty thalasso therapy utilizing freshly pumped seawater pouring from 180 jets. Body wraps incorporate fragrant Hawaiian flowers and healing leaves. There are ten kinds of facials ranging from anti-stress aroma treatments to collagen masks and a signature Chi Yang beauty treatment combining Eastern and Western harmonies. The full venue of health and fitness programs features a workout called "Hip on Hula." Ihilani has 387 luxurious rooms and suites.

The JW Marriott Ihilani Resort and Spa *at Ko Olina fronts eminently swimmable Lagoon One, Kohola (Whale) Lagoon. The multi-award-winning property offers a serene hideaway distinguished by its continued popularity with discriminating Island residents as well as sophisticated travelers from around the world.*

Clockwise, opposite page: Miles of tropically landscaped paths, above, offer runners and walkers perfect places to exercise throughout the resort; a visit to the spa is a vacation experience to sooth the muscles as well as the soul; guests can practice paddling their own canoe or just go along for the ride in the company of the Ko Olina Aloha Team aboard the resort's outrigger.

The Marriott Ko Olina Beach Club includes a spa and children's center, fitness facilities, pool and outdoor barbecue and picnic area. The Marriott Vacation Club International Resort is a complex of two-bedroom holiday villas, each with panoramic views of the Waianae Coast and mountains. The villas are set amidst a fantasia of waterways, pools and tropical gardens bordering Naia, Lagoon Three. The property's decor, signage and exhibits reflect a commitment to an authentic Hawaiian experience.

The Coconut Plantation is a collection of private homes imbued with the tropical graciousness found in the unique Island-style homes of Hawaii's yesteryear sugar barons and plantation managers. The carefully crafted residences are surrounded by luxuriant gardens and have their own swimming lagoon amidst tropical flora.

Private homes at Ko Olina offer living on the golf course in styles from superbly tasteful to privately luxurious. Townhomes of **The Fairways,** *above, were Ko Olina's first residential development.*

Condominium vacation club memberships *like those available through Marriott Vacation Club International are an option at Ko Olina, too. At right, elegantly-designed interiors, created by the renowned architectural firm of Wimberly, Allison, Tong & Goo for the lagoon-front condominums, reflect a committment to an authentic Hawaiian experience.*

More residential developments of exceptional quality, such as Kai Lani at Ko Olina, are planned or underway. Kai Lani will be a private, gated oceanfront condominium of two- and three-bedroom homes. The secluded palm-lined streets and residences are designed to echo the era when island families of status enjoyed private beach estates. The emphasis is on a lifestyle centered around the ocean and its pleasures, with all the amenities of a resort.

The first residential project at Ko Olina was The Fairways, a development of town homes overlooking the second and third fairways of the golf course. With its own pool and lavishly planted gardens, it is home and resort in one.

Knitting the strands of the residential and visitor communities together is a network of tree-lined roads, coastal walking trails, jogging paths and manicured gardens. The tie that binds, however, is the shared spirit of joy.

Above, award-winning two and three-bedroom, one- and two-story condominium homes at **The Coconut Plantation** *offer resort-style living in a private, gated neighborhood amid carefully tended grounds including beautiful gardens, a private neighborhood pool and recreational facilities.*

At left, **Kai Lani at Ko Olina**, *is a private, gated, oceanfront development at the resort that offers the finest in two- and three-bedroom homes in a luxurious style reminiscent of the beachfront retreats favored by Island families in times past.*

Papio and the Shark Goddess of Pearl Harbor

Once, during a time long past, there was a pretty young woman named Papio who was accustomed to being indulged. She often went surfing at a site not far from Pearl Harbor, near where the Ko Olina Marina is now.

One day Papio met an elderly woman who was busy stringing leis made from the beautiful yellow ilima flowers that grow so well in the dry ground around Ko Olina.

"How nice!" said Papio. "A lei like that would certainly look wonderful on me."

The elderly woman, whose name was Koihala, was shocked. It is bad manners to hint for a lei in Hawaii. A lei is the symbol of aloha and should always be freely given. Saying nothing, Koihala continued stringing the delicate yellow blossoms together. She pretended she hadn't heard Papio's rudeness.

"Old woman," said Papio. "Didn't you hear me the first time? One of those yellow ilima leis would look very nice on me!"

Koihala had been working on her leis all morning. After picking more than five hundred of the tiny golden blossoms for each lei, she was sewing them together on a string one by one. Koihala didn't want to give one of her leis to this impertinent girl. "I will make a lei for you some other time," she said, politely, "but these are for my grandchildren. I only have enough blossoms for two leis."

"Hmmph," said Papio. " I haven't time to argue with you!"

Papio dove into the water and had a good time surfing for an hour or two. When she got out she saw that Koihala had finished the gifts for her grandchildren and was getting ready to leave. Papio was overcome with greed.

"I'll take that," she said, snatching one of the leis and putting it around her own neck. "Doesn't that look pretty on me?" Papio gazed with pride at her reflection in a tide pool. Then, so everyone else could admire her, she strode over to a flat rock and stretched out on her back, letting her long hair fall from the edge of the rock into the water.

Now in those days many sharks lived in Pearl Harbor. Their chiefess was Ka-ahupahau, who had been born as a red-headed girl and later turned into a shark. She spent her days watching over the activities of other sharks in Pearl Harbor and keeping an eye on her many human relatives, one of whom was Koihala, the elderly woman.

Ka-ahupahau had been watching Koihala and Papio with some of her shark attendants. When she saw Papio snatch the ilima lei for herself, she was swift to anger as sharks sometimes are.

"Let's teach her a lesson!" she cried, and sent some of her young attendants to grab Papio. They pulled the girl under the sea by her hair where she drowned.

Unfortunately, some of the young sharks also were very hungry. Soon blood from Papio's body ran in the sea. Some of it spilled onto sands near Pearl Harbor that remain stained red to this day.

When Ka-ahuupahau saw the result of her quick temper she was overcome with remorse. She could see that Koihala was upset and frightened, too. Clearly, the punishment was too great for the crime. To make up for what had happened, Ka-ahuupahau decreed that from then on no shark should harm any of the people of Oahu. Because flowers were the cause of the tragedy, she also declared that no one should carry or wear flowers when they go swimming or ride on a boat in the waters of Pearl Harbor.

Oahu

Surprise! Wonder! Even delighted disbelief. These are the only appropriate responses to the island of Oahu. It appears in the ocean almost as a mirage, its skyscrapers rising into flawless blue sky, freeways girding its mountain flanks. Approached by night, Oahu is a cluster of incongruous bright lights in the inky expanse of the Pacific.

The island harbors one of America's great cities, Honolulu, and the world's dream resort, Waikiki. Its suburbs sprawl along the coast, climb the green hills and curl into deep lush valleys. Just over seventy percent of Hawaii's population calls Oahu home. The island is the financial hub of the Pacific, the place where tycoons meet tai-pans in fiber-optic-wired corporate boardrooms.

The island is sophisticated and cosmopolitan. Its lively culture reflects the diversity of the population. Opera, ballet, symphony and theater are all on stage here in season, sharing the spotlight with Japanese Noh, Chinese opera, bagpipes and gamelan. Broadway shows and major stars from several continents schedule Oahu on their world tours.

European designer boutiques, purveyors of precious jade and black pearls, shops specializing in Asian antiquities, fine art galleries and even the big name discounters have opened their doors in this crossroads destination, where shopping is a highly refined and hotly pursued leisure activity.

Restaurants number in the hundreds. Moonlight and mai tais, or French wine and haute cuisine are on Island menus, and so are Continental dining, American fare, and every ethnic flavor from Italian pesto to Indian tandoori. Oahu's Chinese food is reputed to be better than Hong Kong's and ranges from epicurean to take-out. Sushi bars the envy of Tokyo are common, and it's even possible to find kaiseki, the exquisitely presented court food of imperial Japan.

Oahu farmers customize their paradise fields to the needs of the chefs, growing fragrant herbs, sweet fruit and freshest vegetables. Rows of pineapple, banana, coffee, cacao and papaya crops line the coastal plains and the fertile plateau between the Waianae and Koolau mountains. Seafood is raised in ancient fishponds: prawns, mullet and even Caspian sturgeon. This is the other side of Oahu, the barefoot rural country cousin of downtown Honolulu.

The island has beaches with no footprints in the sand, waterfalls singing in the hills, small villages, cattle ranches, vast plantations, and mile after mile of plush green landscape. Parts of Oahu are so wild, no road can completely encircle it. Rugged Kaena Point defies every advance of civilization.

Ko Olina stands at the gateway to this most undeveloped part of Oahu, the Waianae Coast with its miles of splendid beach kissed by ocean waters as clear as a bell. It is the most Hawaiian area of the island, where people still live by traditional Polynesian values and practice the ancient arts of tattoo, wood carving, making kapa (fabric from tree fiber), and feather work. They drop in on modern Oahu only occasionally and often reluctantly. What they value is the aloha spirit passed to them from countless generations. Most of the people who work at Ko Olina and its facilities come from the Waianae Coast. Their natural warmth and hospitality are noted by everyone who visits.

Oahu is the state's capital island and was once the capital of the Kingdom of Hawaii. Today,

Oahu offers a host of activities easily accessible from Ko Olina. **Clockwise, opposite page:** *Lanikai Beach, on the windward shore, is a popular swimming and water sport site for residents and visitors; Iolani Palace in Honolulu's Civic Center—here decked out in patriotic bunting for the birthday of King Kalakaua—is open for tours; Kualoa Ranch offers horseback riding and other ranch activities; Ala Moana Shopping Center, on the edge of Waikiki, offers multiple tiers of shops; Queen Emma Summer Palace displays the beautifully preserved furniture of a 19th century Hawaiian queen.*

At Pearl Harbor, *the white Memorial to the U.S.S. Arizona, right, sunk on December 7, 1941, is visible from the deck of the battleship U.S.S. Missouri on which Japan surrendered at the end of World War II. Both sites offer guided tours.*

lovely Victorian Iolani Palace stands as neighbor to the sleek, modern State Capitol. Iolani Palace, America's only royal residence, has been magnificently restored. Visitors may walk among the crimson and gilt thrones, the royal jewels and portraits, the furnishings and art objects sent by imperial courts of the world as gifts to Hawaiian monarchs. These are the rooms where Hawaii's kingdom reached its greatest flowering and poignant end.

The island's other royal residence, the Queen Emma Summer Palace, sits in the cool uplands of Nuuanu Valley and houses a remarkable collection of Hawaiian furniture executed in native woods. There are also touching reminders of the last days of the Kamehameha dynasty.

Vestiges of the old religion survive at Oahu's temples, most notably Puu O Mahuka Heiau overlooking the surfing beaches of the North Shore, and Kaneaki Heiau in the leafy bowers of Makaha Valley, a few miles from Ko Olina.

Most of Hawaii's top visitor attractions are on Oahu.

America's entry into World War II is commemorated at Pearl Harbor at the Arizona Memorial. A dramatic documentary film chronicles the attack. *The U.S.S. Missouri,* juxtaposed across the bay, has become a museum ship celebrating America's victory. Pearl Harbor, like Ko Olina, was once a part of the *ahupuaa* (ancient land division) of Honouliuli.

Mokolii Island, nicknamed Chinaman's Hat, above, is a popular destination for kayak paddlers off the coast of Kualoa Beach Park, on Oahu's windward side. At top, two young beachgoers savor a refreshing 'shave ice' during an exploring trip in Haleiwa town.

Tahiti, Samoa, Tonga, Fiji and other island nations of Oceania can be visited in one day at the Polynesian Cultural Center in a lacework of lagoons and villages. Shows, dancing, an I-Max theater, luau and evening extravaganza are part of the entertainment.

The world's premier showcase of Hawaii and Pacific cultures is the Bishop Museum in Honolulu. Ancient war god images reside in the shadow of a modern planetarium. The formidable stone museum was erected in 1892 to safeguard the treasures of the Kamehamehas. Contemporary additions have expanded capacity to care for more than half a million cultural artifacts and millions of natural history specimens.

The cultural mix is spiced with action at Waimea Valley Park on Oahu's North Shore. In a valley that was once a center of the Hawaiian religion, authentic prayer towers and thatched temples have been faithfully rebuilt. The arts, crafts, sports, music, dance, and even healing arts of old Hawaii are shared throughout the day. There is also kayaking in Waimea Stream and out into the bay, mountain biking, horseback riding and exploring the hills on all-terrain vehicles. At the head of the valley, a waterfall cascades into a cool plunge pool. The park and its gardens can be toured on foot or by narrated tram tour.

The North Shore's biggest little town is Haleiwa, once the destination of Honolulu vacationers aboard "Dillingham's Folly" railroad. Now Haleiwa is famed as a surfing mecca and art center. The picturesque old wooden buildings house a collection of boutiques, surfer shops, restaurants and galleries. There's also a surfing museum. No drive to the North Shore is complete without a stop in Haleiwa for "shave ice," known in other places as a "snow cone," but available here in flavors such as li hing mui, lilikoi or coconut with ice cream and adzuki beans.

Just a few minutes from Ko Olina, the wet and wild Hawaiian Waters Adventure Park is twenty-five acres of rides, slides and an ocean of aquatic options that include Hurricane Bay where mega waves are guaranteed even when the real Pacific is dozing and lamb-like. There's a special toddler's pool, an adult spa area, food court, family slides and a daring free-fall six-story water slide.

Honolulu's Aloha Tower, at 184 feet, was once the tallest building in Hawaii. Now it presides over a waterfront complex of shops, restaurants and clubs, where cruise ships still call. Nearby, the Hawaii Maritime Center documents Hawaii's long romance with the ocean in a series of inter-active exhibits. Docked out front is the *Falls of Clyde*, the world's last full-rigged four-masted schooner, built in 1898. The pier also is the home of *Hokulea*, the famous voyaging canoe that retraced early Polynesian sea-lanes.

Tucked away in a two-thousand-acre nature preserve overlooking Honolulu, the Hawaii Nature Center encourages families to learn about Oahu's unique environment through hands-on exhibits, hikes and nature walks. The easy Makiki Valley Loop Trail, two and a half miles long, begins at the Center. Among the plants along the trail are the silver-leafed kukui, avocado, guava and mountain apple trees—free samples when fruiting. There are wonderful views of Honolulu looking out to the ocean.

A long time ago, a volcanic cone on the eastern shore of Oahu was breached by the ocean when a seaward wall fell away. The crater became Hanauma Bay, a natural aquarium where swimmers and even novice snorkelers mingle freely with brightly spangled schools of Hawaiian reef fish. Now known as the Hanauma Bay Nature Preserve, it is a marine

Clockwise, from bottom, page 57: Two Japanese-American girls pose in traditional attire in front of Oahu's magnificent Byodo-In Temple, a replica in concrete of an age-old wooden temple in Japan; ancient Hawaiian cord weaving at Polynesian Cultural Center; snorkelers at Hanauma Bay Nature Preserve; dancer presents a modern hula at one of many performances around the island; children examine a pink hibiscus at a leeward Oahu beach.

Clockwise, opposite page: The leeward or West Beach side of Oahu is a year 'round paradise for outdoor activities, offering paddling your own canoe along a sunny shoreline; biking for two in old Haleiwa town; body surfing for beginners as well as professionals; snorkeling in pristine, reef-fish packed seas; or horseback riding along well marked trails in sunny Makaha Valley.

life sanctuary, and the thousands of fish seem to know they are protected as they glide about in their colorful ballets, dancing unperturbed among the swimmers.

The wonderland beneath the waves can be visited without getting wet at Sea Life Park, strategically placed between the mountains and the sea at Makapuu Point. Here, a living coral reef is incorporated into a 300,000-gallon aquarium called The Reef Tank. Marine mammal shows, a restaurant and whaling museum are part of the attraction. It's also home to the world's only wholfin, offspring of a dolphin and whale who met on the job backstage at the park's aquatic theater.

Hawaii's two top pineapple companies show off with attractions. The Dole Pineapple Visitor Center fortifies visitors with fresh-squeezed pineapple juice and sends them out to conquer the world's largest maze. Just down the road, the Del Monte Company maintains its Pineapple Variety Garden bursting with varieties from around the world, including pink pineapple.

Ferns taller than a man, flowers as big as a basketball, orchids smaller than a fingernail are just a few of the amazing flora growing in Oahu's botanical gardens. The rarest flowers in the world have been joined by more than a thousand exotic species brought to the Islands from America, Europe, Asia and Africa. Hawaii's state flower, the hibiscus, blooms in five thousand hybrids. Foster Botanical Garden on the edge of downtown Honolulu has an

award-winning Prehistoric Glen. Jams and jellies made from fruits grown in the garden can be purchased at Lyon Arboretum in Manoa Valley. The Koko Crater Botanical Garden blooms obstinately in a dry volcanic crater. Hoomaluhia Botanical Garden is a 400-acre gem tucked against the crenellated cliffs of the windward Koolau Mountains. It has hiking trails, international gardens and a thirty-two acre lake. For trees, it's the Wahiawa Botanical Garden where sixty specially designated Exceptional Trees shade the winding walkways.

The most famous hike on the island is the climb from the interior crater of Diamond Head to its summit. From there, the panorama of the Waikiki shoreline unfolds in sun-dappled splendor. Beneath the familiar peak of the promontory, powerful Diamond Head Lighthouse beams out across the waves guiding cruise liners and cargo ships to port. The view continues along the palm-fringed coast of Kahala all the way out to Koko Head.

Just getting in a car and driving around Oahu is a rewarding experience. The scenery is breathtaking, the beaches lovely and lonely, and the small towns abound in interesting shops. There are farm stands, prawn farms and roadside restaurants. Around every bend in the road, travelers are ambushed by beauty.

The best part of any Oahu day, however, is coming home to the island within the island, Ko Olina, the Place of Joy.

A Chant of Praise Stops a Massacre

At a time not very long before sea captains from the unknown lands of the West first came to Hawaii, two young men of Oahu went looking for a noble patron. One day Kapaa and his younger brother Kamaka heard that Ku-alii, a great chief, was camped with his army on a plain near Ko Olina.

Kapaa and Kamaka knew that one of Ku-alii's biggest rivals was the chief who ruled Koolauloa, a sacred site on the windward side of Oahu. Maybe, the two brothers thought, they could turn the rivalry between the two chiefs to their own advantage.

"We need to serve a chief who will protect us," said Kapaa, the older brother, "and I want some excitement in my life."

"Ku-alii is the strongest chief in the islands," said Kamaka. "He hasn't lost a battle yet."

"Yes, but how do we get him to accept us? We need to do something to impress him."

Now it happened that the two brothers were not very good warriors. They had no training or experience, and Ku-alii already had an army of 12,000 men ready for his next battle.

What Kapaa and Kamaka did have, however, was the ability to compose chants for the hula. They were experts at creating poetry for the sacred dance of Hawaii.

Suddenly they both had the same idea. "Let's compose a chant for the great Ku-alii!" Kapaa and Kamaka worked hard to create a name chant listing Ku-alii's ancestry back to the gods who created the world.

When their chant was finished it contained many hundred lines of verse listing all of Ku-alii's illustrious feats and ancestors one by one and praising him as a 'messenger from heaven.' Kapaa and Kamaka memorized every line.

Then, as agreed, Kamaka set off for Ku-alii's war camp. There he recited the chief's new name chant. Ku-alii was so impressed that he invited Kamaka to join his army. Thus ingratiated, Kamaka soon asked Ku-alii where he planned to stage his next battle. When Ku-alii indicated a plain near Ko Olina, Kamaka went to the site and marked it with the tail of a fish and a ki leaf.

In the meantime Kapaa journeyed to the Chief of Koolauloa's camp. There he talked the Chief into launching a surprise attack on Ku-alii. That night, with Kapaa, the Chief of Koolauloa led his 1,200 warriors over the Koolau mountains to meet Ku-alii's forces. At dawn they reached the plain near Ko Olina.

As pre-arranged, Kapaa immediately looked for the sign left by his brother. When he found the fish tail and the ki leaf, he ran back to the Chief of Koolauloa.

Pretending to be very worried, Kapaa said, "Oh, great Chief, my brother is with the army of Ku-alii, and he has left me a sign. We are completely surrounded by the 12,000 warriors of your rival's army!"

"What?" cried the Chief. "How can that be?"

"I have an idea," Kapaa said smoothly. "My brother and I composed a name chant for Ku-alii that I could recite. When Ku-alii hears

it, maybe he'll order his army not to attack." The Chief of Koolauloa was no fool. He realized that both he and Ku-alii had been tricked by two very clever brothers, but he also knew that he was outnumbered, so he agreed to Kapaa's idea, but with a warning.

"Chant, Kapaa," he said. "But If you fail to impress Ku-alii and prevent a battle, I'll have you and all your relatives killed!"

The two armies gathered face to face on the plain, 12,000 warriors against 1,200. With such favorable odds Ku-alii's army was spoiling to fight, but before a spear was raised, Kamaka suddenly called out. "Great Chief, isn't that your name chant I hear coming from someone in the enemy's ranks? If the chanter can name your ancestors from beginning to end, shouldn't we show mercy and call off the battle?"

By this time Kapaa was well into the chant. It told in detail of Ku-alii's descent from the great gods and goddesses of Polynesia, and of his many amazing feats. Kapaa's voice was so strong and so beautiful and his words so sure that warriors on both sides stood still to listen. When Kapaa was finished and had named every ancestor correctly, Ku-alii relented. He commanded his army to put down their weapons. No blood was shed that day, but the Chief of Koolauloa had to cede all his lands to Ku-alii.

So the beauty of a Hawaiian name chant prevented a massacre and helped two talented young men acquire a royal patron. Kapaa became a great favorite of Ku-alii, who gave him many gifts of land and food which he shared with his younger brother Kamaka.

Vision

Ko Olina is the oldest and most pristine part of Oahu. It's where the sun always shines, the breeze is at your back, and the ocean gleams and teams with life. The people who live amidst this beauty are Hawaiian in their ways, their hospitality and deep spirituality. They bring these gifts from bygone centuries, and enable Ko Olina to live out its destiny as a place for the fulfillment of joy.

As the new century unfurls its banners, the vision for Ko Olina is that it continue in its ancient designation as a very special sanctuary.

Evolution will continue. Everything that's added will be an enhancement, part of the vision of a thriving, active resort and residential community for the twenty-first century. It is a place to raise children, retire, or sojourn for refreshment of body and spirit. It is a wireless, connected community, close to cities and airport, yet secluded, private, secure. Activities and facilities are designed to help adults and children stretch toward their potential, to make the most of their days, to afford them the leisure to pause and appreciate the simple pleasure of being here. The specially trained Aloha Team makes the vision work. From the gates to the ocean, these men and women care for Ko Olina. They are its ambassadors of aloha, the custodians of beauty, safety and serenity. They are neighbors.

As steward of a unique environment, Ko Olina accepts its responsibilities in water conservation, and respect for the land. The resort is a co-founder of Marine Mammal Watch, guardians of the ocean's creatures. Endangered avifauna are offered hospitable sanctuary. The land is encouraged to bloom and is lovingly tended. The lagoons and beaches are immaculate and inviting.

The vision for the future of Ko Olina must live up to standards set by a long line of Hawaiian kings and queens. It is a sacred commitment to treasure this Place of Joy.

Acknowledgements, Credits and Notes

Mahalo

Many individuals, including several closely associated with Ko Olina Resort, helped to make this book possible. The authors are grateful for the assistance of Jeff Stone, president of Ko Olina Resort Association and resort master developer, John Toner, vice president of Ko Olina Resort Association, Roy Tokujo and Jeanne Murata, Ko Olina Resort Association board members, and Kimberly Wood of Ko Olina Resort Association; Gregg Grigaitis and Rayn Chamizo, Marriott Vacation Club International; Bob Armstrong, Sharlene Yamashita and Nancy Walsh, Kai Lani at Ko Olina; Edward Schoerner and Russell "RD" Doane, Ko Olina Resort & Marina; Donna B. Goth and Nadine T. Lagaso, The Estate of James Campbell; Brad Snyder, Marriott International Inc.; Ken Williams, Ko Olina Community Association; Jim Richerson, Ko Olina Golf Club; Sheila Donnelly Theroux, Robyn Barthelemy and Molly Shackett, Sheila Donnelly & Associates; Lynette "Nettie" Tiffany, Kahu, Lanikuhonua; Kaiula Clark, and members of the Aloha Team who cheerfully posed for photographs.

We would also like to thank members of the Java Writing Group for their review of and contributions to Hawaiian traditional practices and mythology included in the six stories in the book; Bernice Pauahi Bishop Museum Librarian B.J. Short for her assistance with research on the stories; and Tom Parry for his assessment of the original story *How the Reef Fish of Hawaii Got their Colors.*

Additional Photography and Art Credits

Photography:
Jim Ariyoshi, p. 22 left; William "Buzz" Belknap III: pp. 44, bottom, 45 top, 49 top; Vince Cavataio, p. 20; Dave Fleetham: p. 50, Tai Sing Loo: p. 22 top (original image not tinted), Bishop Museum Collection; Eric Nishibayashi: p. 10, 11, 15; Jim Watt: p. 16. Courtesy The Estate of James Campbell: pp. 28, 29, 30, 31 (original photographs on pp. 29, 30, 31 not tinted). Courtesy Ko Olina Resort Association: pp. 2-3, 14, 23, 39, bottom, 43, 44 top, 46 all, 47, 48 top, 49 top. Courtesy Marriott Vacation Club International: p. 48 bottom. Courtesy Kai Lani at Ko Olina: p. 49 bottom. Courtesy Ken Williams: p. 45 bottom.

Original Art:
Michael Furuya: *Mo'o at Pearl Harbor,* p. 40.

Background Notes on the Hawaiian Stories

How the Reef Fish of Hawaii Got Their Colors
© Jodi Parry Belknap

This story is entirely original to the author. It is not based on any previously recorded Hawaiian legend. Elements in it that were inspired by or drawn from traditional Hawaiian practices include those mentioned below.

The *Glossary of Hawaiian Gods* included in some editions of the **Hawaiian Dictionary**, by Mary Kawena Pukui and Samuel Elbert, lists Halelehua as a sea goddess who lives in the channel between the Islands of Oahu and Kauai.

At one time Hawaiians raised a great variety of fish in sea ponds enclosed by stone walls next to the shore. In centuries past the area where Ko Olina is located was renowned for its *ama-ama,* or mullet. One type of ama-ama cultivated here swims around Kaena Point to Laie and back.

Names for children in old and new Hawaii are sometimes received in dreams. In traditional practice a newborn, especially one of higher lineage than his or her parents, may be given to a learned or childless person to raise. Such a child becomes a *hanai,* or adopted son or daughter.

Pueo, Kulia and the Ki Ponds of Ko Olina
© Jodi Parry Belknap

Kulia and his grandfather Konapiliahi are fictional in this original story, but much of what is known about archeological sites and pre-Western history at Ko Olina and the surrounding area is incorporated here.

Ki, or ti plants, and other staple foods once were cultivated extensively in shallow coral sinkholes on the coastal plains of the surrounding land section.

In the 19th century ranchers reported finding stone-covered freshwater springs in the area.

The wetland variety of *kalo,* or taro, was cultivated at Honouliuli, a village in the uplands of the land section to which Ko Olina belongs.

The *pueo,* or indigenous Hawaiian owl, is a revered Hawaiian family *aumakua* or guardian linked to the area. Hawaiian families traditionally made offerings to their aumakua before taking what they needed.

The Hawaiian saying *'Umi 'ia i nui keaho,'* and its English translation, 'Press hard and take a long breath,' is listed in the book **Treasury of Hawaiian Words,** by Harold Winfield Kent, published by the Masonic Public Library of Hawaii, in 1986.

p. 40-41
The Water Lizard and the Pearl Oysters
This version of stories of a *mo-o* and the pearl oysters of Pearl Harbor is based on a 1943 *Hawaiian Historical Society Report* by the renowned Hawaiian historian Mary Kawena Pukui and reprinted in **Sites of Oahu,** by Elspeth P. Sterling and Catherine C. Summers.

p. 50-51
Papio and the Shark Goddess of Pearl Harbor
This story is also adapted from a version recorded by Mary Kawena Pukui in a 1943 *Hawaiian Historical Society* report, and reprinted in **Sites of Oahu,** by Elspeth P. Sterling and Catherine C. Summers. It is part of traditional lore about a special kind of shark that protects people from other sharks in the Islands. In other oral and written retellings the shark goddess herself bites and slays Papio. The cautionary notes when around sharks are obvious.

P. 60-61
A Chant of Praise Stops a Massacre
According to the eminent 20th century cultural historian, Martha Beckwith, legends such as this one about an actual Oahu chief who died in the 18th century are only semi-mythical, and have a strong basis in fact. This story reveals how important poets who could compose long oral chants were in Hawaii—a tradition that is being revived today. Those who would like to know more about this and other Hawaiian beliefs may want to begin by reading Beckwith's book, **Hawaiian Mythology,** published by the University of Hawaii Press.